ISBN 0 85079 121 9

The GAMBOLS

BOOK Nº 31

by Dobs + Barry Appleby

BILL

£1·10

© 1982
Dobs +
Barry
Appleby

PEAS
SEEDS

WOULD YOU SOONER DO SOMETHING ELSE TO-DAY DEAR?

11-4

JUST A MINUTE

I'LL ASK GEORGE

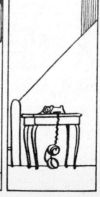

I'LL RING YOU BACK

IT'S GOING TO TAKE ME SOME TIME TO GET THE ANSWER I WANT

© 1981 Dobs + Barry Appleby

2110

GAYE HAS CALCULATED
THAT SHE EATS MORE
DINNERS ON HER LAP
IN FRONT OF THE T.V.
THAN AT A TABLE

© 1982 Dobs + Barry Appleby   2314

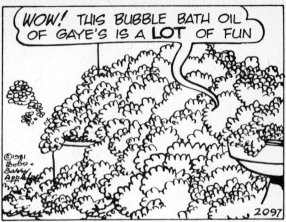

THEY SAY THAT YOU CAN'T TEACH OLD DOGS NEW
TRICKS—BUT FLIVVER AND MIGGY TEACH US
SOMETHING NEW EVERY TIME THEY VISIT US

GAYE'S GREATEST
WISH IS TO HAVE
A ROBOT THAT
WOULD DO ALL
THE CHORES

I NEVER CEASE TO WONDER AT THESE NEW MICRO CHIP INVENTIONS

THIS NEW ONE REGISTERS INCOME — PAYS WAGES — REPLACES AND ORDERS STOCK — RECORDS DELIVERY DATES AND EVEN BUILDS CARS WITHOUT HUMAN ASSISTANCE

AMAZING — BUT CAN IT DO HOUSEWORK?

2256

2223

WELL — I HOPE
I CATCH HIM IN
A GOOD MOOD
SOON

THIS LIST IS
BEGINNING TO GET
RATHER LONG

SUNDAY
JOBS

© 1982
Bobs + Barry Appleby

2-5

DID YOU GET IT TO BURN?

SURE

IT ONLY NEEDED SOME DRY WOOD

© 1982 Dobs + Barry Appleby

2297

GAYE— SHUT THE GATE

© 1981 Dobs + Barry Appleby

2058

COMPUTERS ARE VERY USEFUL—ESPECIALLY IN THE SUPER MARKET

..... AND FURTHERMORE ....

DIAMONDS FOR INVESTMENT

OH! FOR HEAVEN'S SAKE STOP TELLING ME TO BE SENSIBLE

I DON'T **WANT** TO BE SENSIBLE

DIAMONDS FOR INVESTMENT

© 1982. Dobs + Barry Appleby

2280

TELEPHONE

© 1981 Dobs + Barry APPLeby

YOU'D BETTER START DINNER WITHOUT US

TELEPHONE

GEORGE IS IN ONE OF HIS "WE CAN MANAGE ON THREE GALLONS OF PETROL THIS WEEK" MOODS

TELEPHONE

8-11

IT'S THINGS LIKE THIS THAT MAKE GAYE THINK THAT GEORGE WATCHES TOO MUCH TELEVISION

COOEE — I'M HOME

MY! SOMETHING SMELLS GOOD

© 1982 Bob + Barry Appleby 2341

LAST WEEK

THESE CHAIRS NEED RE-UPHOLSTERING

NONSENSE — A WASTE OF MONEY

YESTERDAY

TO-DAY

YOU'RE RIGHT DEAR — THESE CHAIRS DO NEED RE-UPHOLSTERING

© 1981 Bob + Barry Appleby

18-10

843

833

855

835

84-8

943

853

856

GEORGE—WE MUST GET RID OF THAT OLD MATTRESS IN THE LOFT

RIGHT—I'LL FETCH IT DOWN

NOW WHAT DO WE DO WITH IT?

P'RAPS WE COULD SELL IT

WHO WOULD BUY AN OLD THING LIKE THAT?

THE DUSTMAN WON'T TAKE IT

WE CAN'T BURN IT WITH THOSE OLD SPRINGS

WELL THEN—WHAT CAN WE DO WITH IT?

THERE'S ONLY ONE THING

PUT IT BACK IN THE LOFT

862

850

897

831

928

861

'MORNING MRS GRASS

IT'S US... THE GAMBOLS...

....HOME FROM OUR CARAVAN HOLIDAY

© 1982
Dobs + Barry Appleby

2405

HOW DID YOUR FIRST DAY BACK AT WORK GO?

TERRIBLE

DID THE OLD MAN ASK YOU IF YOU'D ENJOYED YOUR HOLIDAY?

NO

HE DIDN'T EVEN NOTICE THAT I'D BEEN AWAY

© 1982
Dobs + Barry Appleby

2406

THESE NEW PERSONAL STEREO RADIOS
MAKE IT HARDER TO "GET THROUGH"
TO THE CHILDREN THAN EVER

HOW OFTEN HAS THIS HAPPENED TO YOU?

2254

1996

GEORGE— HAVE YOU SEEN MY CREDIT CARDS?

SALES START TO-MORROW

© 1982 Bobs + Barry Appleby

2189

I AM **NOT** BEING LAZY

I AM JUST SITTING HERE THINKING TO MYSELF....

WHO AM I TO ADD TO THE POLLUTION OF THE ATMOSPHERE ON A SUNDAY MORNING?

16-5

WHAT IS IT ABOUT WOMEN THAT SO FEW CAN TELL LEFT FROM RIGHT

LOOK GEORGE—SHE'S BOUGHT **ANOTHER** NEW COAT

THEY SPEND MONEY LIKE WATER

YES—BUT THEY HAVE A **HUGE** OVERDRAFT

I WISH **WE** WERE RICH ENOUGH TO AFFORD AN OVERDRAFT

© 1981 Dobs + Barry Appleby 2156

GAYE DAHLING—WOULD YOU AND GEORGE COME AND HAVE A DRINK WITH US BEFORE LUNCH?

© 1982 Dobs + Barry Appleby

THAT WOULD BE LOVELY—THANK YOU

DON'T BOTHER TO CHANGE—JUST COME AS YOU ARE

OH.... AND GAYE DEAR

ASK GEORGE TO BRING HIS OVERALLS

23-5

2214

2155

2318

2027

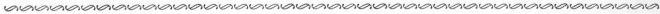

AND SO UNTIL TOMORROW MORNING
IN THE EXPRESS AND SUNDAY EXPRESS
WE SAY "BYE FOR NOW"

© 1982 Dobs + Barry Appleby

Published by Express Newspapers Limited, Fleet Street, London, EC4P 4JT, and printed by Purnell and Sons (Book Production) Ltd., Paulton, Bristol.